Let's Visit New Hope!

By Gayle Goodman & Roy Ziegler

Illustrated by Pat Achilles

For the New Hope Historical Society

In memory of John Alexander Bisignano

Printed in the United States of America
First Printing, 2015
New Hope Historical Society
P.O. Box 41
New Hope, PA 18938
www.newhopehs.org

Hello ! Welcome to New Hope ! My name is Benjamin Parry, but you can call me Ben.

A lot of folks say that I am the Father of New Hope. When my Hope Flour Mill burned down I built a new one and called it New Hope Mill, and they changed the name of our town to New Hope. At my mills we made flour from the wheat grown by farmers. Flour is used to make bread, hamburger rolls, pizza dough and lots of good things to eat !

This is what our town looks like today.

There are no more mills and factories, but it is now a fun place filled with all kinds of shops, restaurants, theaters, parks, and ice cream stores along the historic Delaware River.

Here's how it all started.

William Penn came to America from England way back in 1682 and started a colony that became our state. It was named after William Penn's father.

And there were so many trees growing here that it just made sense to call our new state Pennsylvania. The name means "Penn's Woods."

William Penn also started the city of Philadelphia, which at one time was the capital of the United States. He built his home in the countryside along the Delaware River.

Penn's home in England was called **BUCK**inghamshire so he called his new home in America **BUCKS** County. You can visit Pennsbury Manor, William Penn's home, where peacocks roam the grounds !

New Hope is located in beautiful Bucks County.

When you come to New Hope, there are many things you can do.

Walk through town and see the fun shops.

Play on the cannon from the
American Civil War . . .

. . . but don't try to lift the cannon balls !

Check out the ten-foot tall Lenape Indian chief on the lawn of my beautiful Parry Mansion.

The Lenni-Lenape Native American Indians settled in this area hundreds of years before William Penn arrived. Their ancestors were living here thousands of years ago !

Eat ice cream . . .
There are many ice cream shops and fun flavors !

Go see the old, restored train station. Take a ride through the Bucks County woods and forests, and over the creeks and streams that were once used to run the old mills.

Stop at the local book store and see why it is called the "bookshop with a personality."

See the Christmas shop that is open all year long.

And don't worry if you get hungry . . .

. . . there are so many restaurants in New Hope that you will have a hard time deciding where to go.

There are many mule statues
around New Hope and
Bucks County.
That's because in the old days
the mules pulled canal boats along
the Delaware Canal.
The boats carried coal, lumber
and farm products from the mines
and farms to New Hope
and Philadelphia.
That was very important to
our growing country.

Today you can ride your bike
or hike along the same towpaths
where the mules walked
long ago.

Here are some mule statues painted by Bucks County artists. The last one is blank for you to color your own mule !

Now . . . check out the Delaware River.
I, Ben, was responsible for building the first
bridge across the Delaware River to
Lambertville more than 200 years ago.

Today you can cross the same
river on a ferry boat or go
tubing and canoeing !

George Washington crossed the Delaware on Christmas night, 1776 and defeated the British army in Trenton just a few miles down the river. You can visit Washington Crossing State Park on Christmas Day and watch a very realistic reenactment of Washington's crossing . . . but make sure to wear a warm coat, hat and gloves.

Many people don't know that General Washington also crossed right here in New Hope with his whole army.

Because of these crossings, New Hope and Bucks County were very important in the Revolutionary War.

And George Washington was such a successful general that he later became the first president of the United States !

OUR FIRST PRESIDENT

Just a few miles south of New Hope on River Road, at Bowman's Hill Wildflower Preserve in Solebury, you can hike or just stroll among the ponds and thousands of beautiful trees and native plants.

Nearby you will want to go up 100 feet to the top of the Bowman's Hill Tower where you can see for many miles around . . .

. . . and see what it might have looked like
when William Penn arrived !

Farther down River Road you can visit Washington Crossing Historic State Park. In the summertime you can go to the Open Air Theater and watch live shows like "Big" or "Seussical" or "The Wizard of Oz."

If you and your family will be here for a few days, you can visit Peddler's Village and Giggleberry Fair. Little kids can ride the Grand Carousel and big kids can play on Giggleberry Mountain.

Also visit Doylestown, where you can tour the beautiful Michener Museum. It was built in the old Bucks County jail. And walk across the street to the Mercer Museum where there are more than 4,000 artifacts . . . strange, interesting, and fun !

Then just down the road you can visit Green Hill Farm, headquarters of Pearl S. Buck International. They help children in other parts of the world by sending donations for school, clothes and food. You can see the home of Pearl S. Buck, the famous author of many best-selling books including "The Good Earth." Many Americans learned about China for the first time from this book.

How about a balloon ride ?
See the Delaware River . . .
See the
beautiful mountains . . .
See nature . . .
See the people
in New Hope
and Bucks County . . .
. . . all from high up in the air !
It's magical !

Back in New Hope,
stop by the Bucks County
Children's Museum to play
at the Factory Works . . .

. . . and dig for dinosaur bones . . .

. . . and
learn
about
the wind.

If you visit New Hope in the spring, be sure to walk across the bridge to Lambertville for the exciting Shad Festival.

In June, your family will love the New Hope Historical Society's colorful garden tour.

If you visit in May, *New Hope Celebrates* has a rainbow parade and more food, music and ice cream !

On the Fourth of July go to Tinicum Park, just a few miles north of New Hope, to celebrate America's birthday with beautiful music, delicious picnics and fantastic fireworks !

Another wonderful place to visit in New Hope is the Bucks County Playhouse, located just across the street from the Parry Mansion which was my home. The Playhouse was once the building where my New Hope Mill was located, and today it is a busy theater with many different events all year long.

The Playhouse has special programs for kids, too. In the summer, teens audition, learn a play, and perform it for their family, friends and the general public . . . so you can see it too.

In September, go to the New Hope Arts and Crafts Festival where there will be many artists and craftspeople showing their work. And guess what . . . more food, music and ice cream !

In the fall you can take a scary Ghost Tour around New Hope and see some of the spookiest places in town !

BOO!

Now you know about some of the history and fun things to do in New Hope.

And you know about some of the interesting things to do in nearby towns and some of the great history of Bucks County.

Come visit New Hope !

1837
NEW HOPE

Come visit us!

The New Hope Historical Society welcomes you to Benjamin Parry's Mansion at 45 South Main Street in New Hope. The mansion is open every weekend from May through October for personalized tours by our knowledgeable docents. And take a walking tour of historic New Hope to visit all the places you have read about in this book.

Call us at 215-862-5652 to arrange a group tour or email us at newhopehs@verizon.net. You can also check us out on our website at www.newhopehs.org.

Acknowledgements

Thank you to Mrs. Schollin's 2012-13 second grade class at the New Hope-Solebury Lower Elementary School. You were the inspiration for this book !

Thank you to Kelly Schollin and Peg Logan, elementary teachers extraordinaire, for making sure we stayed appropriately focused on the kids.

Thank you to illustrator and designer Glenn Zimmer for his help with the production of this book.

Thank you to the Bucks County Conference and Visitors Bureau.

And . . . thank you to Jim Searing, Chuck Tarr, and George Achilles . . . just because.

About the Authors

Gayle Goodman has lived, worked, and visited all over the world, and now resides in Solebury, Pennsylvania, the town right next to New Hope. She serves on the Board of Directors of the New Hope Historical Society and of Pearl S Buck International, and volunteers in the New Hope-Solebury Elementary School. Gayle loves the beauty, history, arts, friends, restaurants, and ice cream of Bucks County.

Roy Ziegler is the author of two books about New Hope history: *New Hope, Pennsylvania: River Town Passages* traces the history of 50 New Hope buildings as far back as 300 years, and *The Parrys of Philadelphia and New Hope* chronicles four generations of the dynamic Parry Family. His novel, *Twilight of Separation* is a coming of age novel set during the social turbulence of the 1960s. Roy is past president of the New Hope Historical Society and serves on the Society's board of directors.

Pat Achilles painted the illustrations of all the interesting and colorful places around New Hope for this book. Ever since she was in grade school she has loved to draw and paint. She likes reading about history, music, theater and art, and enjoys learning even more by visiting historic places and going to concerts, plays and art shows. To see other books Pat has illustrated, look on her website www.achillesportfolio.com.

Made in the USA
Charleston, SC
05 February 2015